Shapes In Nature

Welcome, Little Explorer! ●🔍

Welcome:

Nature is full of surprises, and one of its most amazing secrets is how it uses shapes! Have you ever noticed how some things in nature look a lot like the shapes you learn in school? From the round sun above to the spirally shells on the beach, there's a whole world of shapes waiting for you to discover.

About Your New Book:

Ready for a shape hunt? ● From everyday shapes to nature's unique wonders, let's uncover why bees adore hexagons and where stars shine on Earth. Dive in, and see how nature dazzles as the ultimate artist! ✣★🐚

Let's Explore Together:

1. <u>Spot the Shape!</u> As you turn each page, try to spot the shape we're talking about before reading about it. Make it a fun game!
2. <u>Ask and Answer:</u> After reading, answer the interactive questions. They're a fun way to see what you've learned!
3. <u>Draw and Discover:</u> Got some crayons or colored pencils? Why not draw the shapes you find in this book in your own special way?

Remember, there's no right or wrong way to explore. Just open your eyes, be curious, and see how many shapes you can discover in the world around you!

Happy exploring! 🌿🔍☀

A Fun Fact

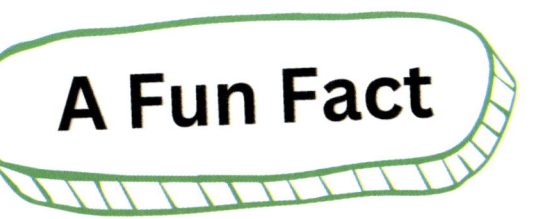

🐝 Honeycomb Fact: Bees build with hexagons, those cool six-sided shapes, because they fit perfectly and save wax. Every honeycomb shows just how clever bees are! 🐝🐝

An orange and pink sunset with kids pointing at the circular sun.

CIRCLE SUNSETS

Sunsets are often seen in a beautiful circular shape, like a big, colorful ball in the sky.

DID YOU KNOW?

The sun looks round because it's a sphere!

QUESTION:

Have you seen a circle sunset?

GLOSSARY

Sphere: A perfectly round 3D shape.

A youngster lounging on the turf, admiring the hexagon-shaped constellations.

STARRY HEXAGONS

When you look closely at some star patterns, they can form a hexagon shape in the sky.

DID YOU KNOW?

Bees use hexagons to build their honeycombs!

QUESTION:

Can you draw a hexagon?

GLOSSARY

Hexagon: A shape with six straight sides.

A young hand showcasing a helical seashell.

SPIRAL SEASHELLS

Seashells often have a spiral shape, twirling around and around.

DID YOU KNOW?

Some animals like snails live inside these spiral homes!

QUESTION:

Ever counted the twirls of a seashell?

GLOSSARY

Spiral: A shape that winds around a center point.

An aerial view of verdant rectangular plots with children frolicking.

RECTANGLE FIELDS

Big fields where farmers grow food can look like rectangles from high above.

DID YOU KNOW?

Rectangle shapes are everywhere, from doors to books!

QUESTION:

Can you find 3 rectangle things at home?

GLOSSARY

Rectangle: A shape with four straight sides.

A youngster presenting heart-formed leaves beneath a towering tree.

HEART-SHAPED LEAVES

Some trees have leaves that look just like hearts.

DID YOU KNOW?

People give heart shapes to show love.

QUESTION:

Can you spot a heart shape around you?

GLOSSARY

Heart shape: A shape that looks like the symbol of love.

An adventurer scaling a petite triangle-topped summit.

TRIANGULAR PEAKS

Mountains often end in triangular peaks, pointing up to the sky.

DID YOU KNOW?

The pyramids in Egypt are also big triangles!

QUESTION:

Have you seen a triangle mountain?

GLOSSARY

Peak: The top part of a mountain.

Young eyes observing a bird's nest cradling elliptical eggs.

OVAL EGGS

Many birds lay oval-shaped eggs. They're a bit longer than a circle.

DID YOU KNOW?

Not all eggs are the same size. Ostriches lay the biggest eggs!

QUESTION:

Can you draw an oval?

GLOSSARY

Oval: A shape that looks like a stretched circle.

A procession of ants advancing towards sustenance.

LINE OF ANTS

Have you seen ants moving in a straight line? They're following each other!

DID YOU KNOW?

Ants follow a scent trail laid down by other ants to find food!

QUESTION:

Can you walk in a straight line like ants?

GLOSSARY

Scent: A smell.

Youthful joy creating round wave patterns in splashy puddles.

CIRCULAR RAINDROPS

When it rains, each drop makes a little circle when it lands on water.

DID YOU KNOW?

Every raindrop is like a tiny circle falling from the sky.

QUESTION:

Have you played in the rain?

GLOSSARY

Circle: A round shape with no corners.

Children in a garden, captivated by a cactus sporting quadrate textures.

SQUARE PATCHES

Some plants, like certain cacti, have square-shaped sections on them.

DID YOU KNOW?

Chessboards are squares too, and we play games on them!

QUESTION:

Have you seen a square shape in your garden?

GLOSSARY

Square: A shape with four equal sides.

GLOSSARY

Circle: A round shape with no corners.
Sphere: A perfectly round 3D shape. It's like a ball that you can hold!
Hexagon: A shape with six straight sides. It has more sides than a square!
Spiral: A shape that winds around a center point. Imagine twirling a ribbon around your finger!
Rectangle: A shape with four straight sides. Two of its sides are longer than the other two.
Heart shape: A shape that looks like the symbol of love. Think of the drawings you see on Valentine's cards!
Peak: The top part of a mountain. It's like the mountain's pointy hat!

A SPECIAL NOTE

Hello Wonderful Explorers! ✺

Did your little shape detective enjoy discovering the magical patterns in nature with us? Here at Biotic Chronicles, we adore unveiling the wonders of the world in the most delightful way. Your insights and stories light up our day!

If you can, please take a moment to share your thoughts on Amazon or wherever you got this book. Your feedback not only helps other explorers find our tales but also fuels our passion for creating more adventures that spark imagination.

Thank you for being a part of the Biotic Chronicles adventure. Keep observing, keep dreaming, and always cherish your enchanting journeys!

With all my best,

Dr. Amit Khanna
Founder, Biotic Chronicles

About the Author

Dr. Amit Khanna is a distinguished molecular biologist and a storyteller at heart. With a rich background in genomics, he navigates the intricate dance of molecules, genes, and DNA. But for Amit, it's more than just the science; it's the stories that lie hidden within our genetic code, the tales that nature has silently penned down over eons.

While many are content with the black and white of scientific data, Dr. Khanna sees a vivid tapestry of narratives. Beyond his research, he has a unique talent for narrating science in a way that captivates, educates, and inspires. He brings the wonders of the molecular world to life, making it accessible and fascinating for audiences of all ages.

Whether it's through his books or his engaging science narrations, Dr. Khanna's mission is to bridge the gap between complex biological phenomena and the curious minds eager to understand them.

To learn more about his narrations, explorations, and the world of biology through his lens, visit www.BioticChronicles.com.

Dive Deeper with Biotic Chronicles!

For a delightful collection of books tailored for children aged between 5 and 15 years old, as well as exclusive behind-the-scenes content, downloadable coloring pages, and engaging monthly newsletters, chart your course to www.BioticChronicles.com. Immerse yourself in the magical and scientific realms waiting to be explored!

Exclusive activities! 🎉 🐸

Become a part of our Birthday Club and enjoy special messages and book discounts on your special day. 🎊 Dive into our Readers' Theater and grab script versions of our stories - perfect for enacting on your playful days!

Visit www.BioticChronicles.com

Copyright Notice:

All rights reserved. No part of this book may be reproduced or transmitted in any form or by any means, electronic or mechanical, including photocopying, recording, or any information storage and retrieval system, without prior written permission from the publisher.

Made in the USA
Las Vegas, NV
27 October 2023